THE ESSENTIALS
OF BONSAI

THE ESSENTIALS
OF BONSAI

By the Editors of Shufunotomo

Introduction by Donald Richic

TIMBER PRESS

Portland, Oregon

Published in cooperation with American Horticultural Society

Timber Press
P.O. Box 1631
Beaverton, OR 97075
ISBN #0-917304-27-6

First printing, 1982
Second printing, 1984
Third printing, 1985
Fourth printing, 1986

Printed in Japan

Contents

Preface 5
Introduction *by Donald Richie* 7
Bonsai Masterpieces 13–24, 73–84

1. The Pleasure of Growing Bonsai 25

2. Bonsai Styles................................26

   Classification of Styles   *26*
   (1) According to the shape of the trunks   *26*
   (2) According to the number of trunks   *28*
   (3) According to the shape of the roots   *29*
   (4) According to the shape of the branches   *30*
   (5) According to composition   *31*

3. Appreciation of Bonsai 32

   Front and Rear Sides   *32*
   Exposed Roots (*Nebari*)   *33*
   Tachiagari (Lower part of the trunk)   *34*
   Trunk and Bark   *34*
   Yaku-eda and *Imi-eda*   *35*

4. Plants Suitable for Bonsai 38

5. Raising Bonsai 39

   Collecting Wild Seedlings   *39*
   Raising Bonsai from Seed   *44*
   Raising Bonsai from Cuttings   *46*
   Layering   *48*
   Grafting   *50*
   Dividing   *52*

6. Care of Bonsai 54

    Tools and Equipment   *54*
    Repotting   *55*
    Soils   *59*
    Placement   *60*
    Watering   *62*
    Fertilizer   *64*
    Pests   *65*

7. Training Bonsai 66

    Pinching Buds   *66*
    Leaf Cutting   *68*
    Pruning   *69*
    Wiring   *71*

8. How to Shape Bonsai Styles 85

    Pruning the Branches and Twigs   *86*
    Deciding upon Root Placement   *87*
    Trimming the Roots   *87*
    Preparing the Pot   *88*

9. Practical Techniques 90

    Single Trunk   *90*
    Cascade Style   *93*
    Group Plantings   *96*
    Rock Planting   *100*
    Herbs and Grasses   *104*

    Index............107

Preface

So far Shufunotomo has published about 50 titles on bonsai in the Japanese language, and this book is based on materials obtained from these publications. Bonsai is an art closely related to nature and, as such, abounds with variety. Not only are there numerous different plant species to be cultivated as bonsai, but each individual tree has its own characteristics. While the particular methods of growing and caring for the trees differ according to the natural circumstances, there are some fundamental principles which remain constant. This book offers the essentials of bonsai to those who would like to get started and to those who already have some experience in this fascinating field.

We are very grateful to Mr. Yoshio Takayanagi, who helped us compile this book. He is a free-lance writer on bonsai and has edited several books on the subject. We also appreciate the assistance of both Mrs. Kiyo Inoue, who translated the original Japanese text into English and Mrs. Dale Hilton, who made additional suggestions about the manuscript.

Introduction

By Donald Richie

A *bon* is a tray or salver, *sai* is a dependent noun meaning "grow," and the word *bonsai* means something growing in a shallow container, a tree in a pot. The emphasis, it will be noted, is upon living and growing, the nuance is that the bonsai is entirely natural.

When the West speaks of bonsai it uses the term "dwarfed tree," and at once a difference in attitude between East and West becomes apparent. The nuance is that something has been made less than normal, perhaps even less than natural. We assume that the bonsai is stunted, made other than it might have been. They, the Japanese, assume that the small size of the tree increases rather than decreases our appreciation of the nature inherent in it.

These different assumptions become apparent when we compare the Japanese bonsai with the only Western form of tree training—the espaliered tree. Here, the branches are pulled to right-angle positions with the trunk, the form itself is diminished and the purpose of such a tree is to create the man-made geometry which, in the classical Western garden, is the ideal.

A comparison of garden ideals between the two cultures will help define the Japanese attitude toward the bonsai itself. In the Japanese garden the premise is that nature is to be revealed. It is always there, but some rocks must be moved, a vista opened, a tree planted, before this nature can be properly seen and appreciated. Man at the most merely tidies. He does not create.

The difference in attitude seen in the Western classical garden is apparent. Here trees are put into rows and flowers into beds. The vista is not only man-made, it is man-conceived as well. This view is balanced, geometrical and is meant to be seen but from a single point-of-view, that of the man standing and looking at it. It is nature tamed rather than nature revealed.

Western man has long assumed that he is the lord of creation and that, god-like, he may create his own ideals. The traditional Japanese assumes that he is a part of nature itself and hence shares its qualities. Human-like, he assists nature. One contradicts and improves upon nature; the other agrees with and reveals nature. Both manipulate, but their assumptions in so doing are quite separate.

This accepted, one must also point out that in fact the Japanese do change nature to an extent when they miniaturize trees and create bonsai. Yet, even here, the larger attitude is apparent. The Japanese miniaturize a tree so that it will retain, in smaller form, all the natural properties and conform to nature. But why miniaturize it in the first place?

The Japanese taste for miniaturization—which is very real, as real for electronic circuitry as it is for bonsai—seems to base itself upon the proposition that to make small is make understandable. The Western idea of the small as being quaint and curious is not that of the Japanese. Perhaps to make small is indeed to make lovable but only because the result is more understandable. When bonsai were first seen by the West in any number, at the London Exposition of 1909, the Western notion that the little trees were dwarfed, that they were quaint and eccentric surprised the Japanese. They had been thinking of their bonsai in a very different manner. Just how they had been thinking of them is indicated by the history of bonsai in Japan.

The garden is, of course, also a miniaturization, and the Japanese were making gardens well over a thousand years ago. Just when the art of the bonsai made its appearance is debated but it is genrally agreed that, like gardening itself, it came from China—perhaps as early as fifteen hundred years ago. There, it is said, men discovered trees naturally miniaturized trees—small but perfectly mature juniper growing on rock faces, for example—admired them, brought them home and potted them. Something of the sort may well have occured in Japan, either naturally or in emulation of the Chinese models.

The first Japanese recorded reference to bonsai is in a scroll by Takane Takashina dated 1309 and called the *Kasuga-gongen-genki*. In it a small potted tree is pictured. There are, however, earlier hear-say references. It is said that Honen Shonin (1133–1212), a revered Buddhist figure, was a bonsai enthusiast and there is a much later scroll showing his collection.

Certainly by the fourteenth-century bonsai were among the decorations to be found on the Buddhist altar. Along with ikebana, bonsai were thus regarded as fitting. Nature—in Buddhism as in Shinto—was on object for reverence. Man merely shaped the divine, he did not create it.

It is but a single step from the Buddhist altar to the *tokonoma* alcove of the home. In both places the bonsai is an object of a kind of reverence. Certainly, in the home the small tree stood for an attitude toward nature which was non-anthropomorphic and, to that extent, transcendent.

Further, the bonsai became a paradigm for that attitude toward nature which is seen not only in traditional Japanese gardening but in traditional Japanese architecture as well—where the inside is a part of the outside and vice-versa, where the house is part of the garden (or the surrounding nature) and the garden is also part of this house. This symbolization of the symbiotic relationship existing between man and nature has actually been one of the qualities of Japanese life until quite recently. Indeed, one of the reasons for the continuing miniaturization of trees might have been to make them small enough to fit inside the dwelling.

At the same time, however, there is no denying that a tendency which, conversely, attempted to divorce natural objects from their natural contexts (a tendency finally triumphant in contemporary Japan) began to be noticed. It was noticed as early as in the *Tsurezuregusa* of Yoshida Kenko (1283–1351). In it he writes that "to appreciate and find pleasure in curiously curved potted trees is to love deformity." Yoshida was, to be sure writing only of the enthusiasm for bonsai, not of its appreciation. Nonetheless, it is easy to imagine the fourteenth-century connoisseur being precious over the matter of rare miniature trees.

Rare and valuable it would appear. The next bonsai reference, that of a Noh play by Seami (1363–1444), insists upon their being expensive. In *Hachi-no-Ki* (literally, *A Tree in a Pot*), the impoverished old man destroys his remaining bonsai to make a fire to warm his distinguished guest. The destruction of beauty and rarity for a noble purpose may have been one of the points of the drama, but beauty and rarity also make for expense.

Also indicated is that, around this time, bonsai were being collected not as nature but as art objects—or else the old man would have had nothing to make his warming bonfire with. Shortly, therefore, various bonsai schools and bonsai masters appeared. By the beginning of the Tokugawa period (1600), the art was codified, as was that of ikebana. The third Tokugawa shogun, Iemitsu (1604–1651) was himself a noted bonsai afficiando, and had his own collection. There is even now in the Imperial Palace, nearly five hundred years later, a five-needled pine bonsai, still flourishing, of which he was said to have been particularly fond.

During the Tokugawa period itself, there also appeared a number of bonsai catalogues. One of the first specialists was a scholar named Ito Ibei. The printmaker Kiyoharu (fl. 1725) made several prints of his collection. Finally, in 1803, the first catalogue of bonsai, the *Kinsei-Jufu*, was complied.

We have thus, in the history of bonsai in Japan, a natural object, made small for aesthetic reasons and, eventually, for commercial purposes as well. From nature-worshiping we have proceeded to nature-loving and finally to naturemerchandizing. Running through this history, and continuing until now, however, is the idea that it is nature itself, nature merely touched up, as it were, which is to be admired. There is the assumption, still present in Japan, of the multiplicity of "natural" nature. Each tree is different and none are identical. Each therefore has its own worth and, consequently, its own value. And the value can be high. A thousand year old juniper, if such can be found, would cost up to fifty million yen, which is about a quarter of a million dollars.

That bonsai is a business cannot be denied but it should also be remembered that the business rests upon a singular assumption, one which is at any rate singular-seeming to the West. When we admire a bonsai we are admiring age, an antiquity which by comparison with our own brief span seems eternal. We are also admiring, in a smaller and hence more understandable form, nature itself. The bonsai is a portable cosmos. It is, precisely, a microcosm, containing within it, unchanged in everything but size, the mystery of the universe. We properly feel humble before the tree in the pot. We encourage it to express itself, we help it, we assist and aid. And in this way we—even we of the fragmented West—are made whole again by taking our own proper position within the barely understood scheme of nature itself.

Donald Richie
Tokyo, 1981

Bonsai Masterpieces

Five-needle pine (*Pinus parviflora* Sieb. et Zucc.)
80 years old, 90 cm (2'11''), *Moyogi*

Japanese black pine (*Pinus thunbergii* Parl.)
30 years old, 30 cm (1'), *Ishi-tsuki*

Maple (*Acer palmatum* Thunb. var. *matumurae* Makino)
30 years old, 50 cm (1'7''), *Moyogi*

Five-needle pine (*Pinus parviflora* Sieb. et Zucc.)
50 years old, 80 cm (2'7''), *Netsuranari*

Needle juniper (*Juniperus rigida* Sieb. et Zucc.
80 years old, 70 cm (2'4''), *Moyogi*

Japanese zelkova (*Zelkova serrata* Makino)
30 years old, 30 cm (1'), *Hokidachi*

Maple (*Acer palmatum* Thunb. var. *matumurae* Makino)
30 years old, 30 cm (1′), *Yose-ue*

Sasanqua tea (*Camellia sasanqua* Thunb.)
20 years old, 55 cm (1'9''), *Moyogi*

Metasequoia (*Metasequoia glyptostroboides* Hu et Cheng)
10 years old, 90 cm (2'11''), *Moyogi*

Needle juniper (*Juniperus rigida* Sieb. et Zucc.)
Yarrow (*Achillea sibirica* Ledeb.)

Japanese red pine (*Pinus densiflora* Sieb. et Zucc.)
Maple (*Acer palmatum* Thunb. var. *matumurae* Makino)
Needle juniper (*Juniperus rigida* Sieb. et Zucc.)
Azalea (*Rhododendron molle* G. Don var.)
Dwarf ilex (*Ilex serrata* Thunb. var. *subtilis* Loes.)
Selaginella (*Selaginella involvens* Spring.)

23

Star jasmine (*Trachelospermum jasminoides* Lem.)
50 years old, 30 cm (1'), *Han-kengai*

1. The Pleasure of Growing Bonsai

Bonsai is an art which expresses in miniature the beauty of natural tree forms. A single tree in a pot can suggest a striking element of landscape. Yet the aim of bonsai is to interpret rather than copy nature. It is a "living sketch" in which aesthetic qualities of the plant are made prominent through careful cultivation.

As a living work of art, the bonsai tree changes from season to season. Buds sprout in early spring, followed by summer's cooling green foliage. The autumn brings rich color to the leaves and winter reveals the tasteful shape of a bare tree. Bonsai brings such seasonal joy close all year through. This, indeed, is one of the many pleasures of working with bonsai as one encourages the growth of appealing forms.

2. Bonsai Styles

Bonsai are classified in several ways. The main categories or styles are based on the general shape of the tree in the pot. Other identifications refer to the position and number of trunks, the shape of the roots and branches, and the type of composition. The styles derive from growth patterns observed in the natural environment. While trees of a particular style resemble each other in form, each has unique characteristics which add great variety and enjoyment to this art.

The following is a list of styles used in bonsai circles. Knowledge of such standard styles is helpful in growing your own bonsai or in simply appreciating the beauty of bansai.

Classification of Styles

(1) According to the shape of the trunks

Formal Upright (*chokkan*):

This tree has a single straight trunk, which tapers upward. The roots spread in all directions at the base. Ideally, the branches should be well spaced and symmetrically balanced front and rear, and left and right.

Chokkan
Yesso spruce

Moyogi
Japanese black pine

Shakan
Japanese black pine

Kengai
Sargent juniper

Bankan
Japanese black pine

Bunjingi
Five-needle pine

Informal Upright (*moyogi*):

The trunk may be curved and may grow at a slight slant. The apex of the tree remains directly over the base.

Slanting (*shakan*):

The trunk has a slant either to the left or right with the branches growing on both sides of the tree.

Cascade (*kengai*); **Semi-cascade** (*han-kengai*):

The cascading tree has an arched trunk with the foliage "spilling" in a graceful line below the bottom of the pot. Like the cascade, the semi-cascade trunk grows upward and then turns downward, but at a less abrupt angle. The foliage of the semi-cascade need not reach below the pot.

Coiled (*bankan*):

The trunk is extremely crooked, in some cases entwined around itself.

Literati (*bunjingi*):

This style features a slender trunk with sparse branches usually grouped at the top. Its tone is of quiet elegance.

Twisted (*nejikan*):

The whole trunk is twisted. The twist may originate from natural causes either as a genetic characteristic of the tree or from the environment.

Nejikan
Pomegranate

(2) According to the number of trunks

Single-trunk (*tankan*)

Twin-trunk (*sokan*):

The trunk is divided into two at the base of the tree, with one trunk larger or thicker than the other. The *sokan*, *sankan*, *gokan*, and *kabudachi* are all styles in which multiple trunks grow from a single root.

Three-trunk (*sankan*); **Five-trunk** (*gokan*):

The *sankan* is divided into three and the *gokan* into five.

Tankan
Yesso spruce

Sankan
Five-needle pine

Kabudachi
Five-needle pine

Neagari
Five-needle pine

Netsuranari
Sargent juniper

Ikadabuki
Five-needle pine

Clump (*kabudachi*):

This style features a cluster of trunks which stand very close together as they grow from a single root.

(3) According to the shape of the roots

Exposed root (*neagari*):

The roots of this bonsai are exposed, growing out of the ground. The bare roots make the tree look as if it has endured years of severe weathering.

Sinuous (*netsuranari*):

The numerous trees look as if they have individual roots, but actually, they grow from a single root, which weaves about under the soil.

Raft (*ikadabuki*):

The name comes from its raft-like shape. What looks like multiple trunks are actually branches that have grown from a trunk buried on its side under the soil. This type is similar to the *netsuranari*, but trees of the *ikadabuki* style usually grow in a straight line, while those of *netsuranari* form a curved line.

(4) According to the shape of the branches

Broom (*hokidachi*):

The shape of this style resembles a broom turned upside down. Numerous small branches fan out from the tree starting near the middle of the main trunk.

Wind-swept (*fukinagashi*):

All the branches lean in one direction as if driven by strong winds. Similar trees can be found growing naturally in particularly windy places such as the seashore.

Extended (*sashieda*):

A single-trunk tree with a large branch, which extends quite far in one direction.

Sashieda
Japanese apricot

Hokidachi
Zelkova

Fukinagashi
Five needle pine

(5) According to composition

Group planting (*yose-ue*):

Composed of a group of trees planted in a shallow tray to create the effect of natural scenery.

Rock-grown (*ishitsuki*):

In this style a tree is used in combination with a rock to suggest a landscape. There are two kinds of *ishitsuki*. In one the tree is planted directly upon the rock and in the other the roots of the tree are trained to grow over the rock as they reach down into the soil.

Yose-ue
Maple

Ishitsuki
Maple

The Front of the Tree   The Back of the Tree

3. Appreciation of Bonsai

Front and Rear Sides

Bonsai are viewed from the front. It is therefore important for the bonsai grower to decide which side of the tree to use as the front. This should be determined by placing the tree at eye level and examining it from all angles. One should select the most pleasing view based upon the total effect of the roots, trunk, and large branches. That is, the side with the most potential for showing the structure of the tree to its best advantage.

According to the style in which the tree is to be trained there are some general rules concerning the position of the main branches with respect to the front and back. For the style which you choose make sure the tree has the proper number of branches on the front. It is also important that the apex of the tree leans forward toward the viewer.

Exposed Roots *(Nebari)*

The roots of young trees growing in the wild are hidden under the ground. Gradually these roots are exposed as the tree ages. Roots seen firmly embracing the earth beneath them give the tree an aura of great maturity. The exposed roots, called *nebari*, are one of the most important elements in judging bonsai. There are three varieties of *nebari*;

Shiho-Happo Nebari (in all directions)

The main roots spread out in all directions, creating a sense of stability and offering a pleasing variety of spacing and root sizes. The *nebari* style is highly regarded in bonsai.

Bankon (rock-like roots)

As the *shiho-nebari* grow and develop, the roots weave tightly together and look like one single mass. This style is unusual and very impressive.

Kata-nebari (one-sided root)

In this case the main root develops to one side. Though not generally considered as desirable as *shiho-nebari*, this style can be used to give balance to slanting or cascade style trees. The asymmetry of this style gives the impression of natural forms.

Bankon

Shiho-Happo Nebari

Kata-nebari

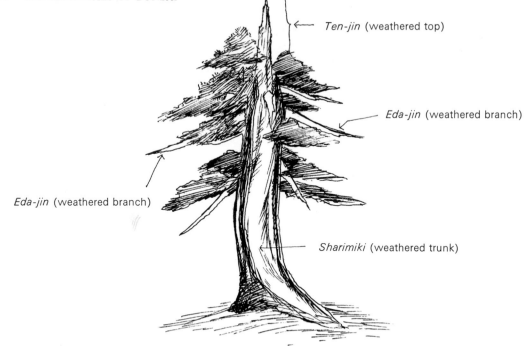

Ten-jin (weathered top)

Eda-jin (weathered branch)

Eda-jin (weathered branch)

Sharimiki (weathered trunk)

Tachiagari (Lower part of the trunk)

The section of the trunk from the base to the lowest branch is called *tachiagari*. This area is considered very important in a single trunk bonsai. In cascade or clump styles it is of less significance. The *tachiagari* should be thick at the base of the trunk and then taper upward. As a whole, a simple but powerful shape is desirable.

Trunk and Bark

Among the most pleasing shapes for trunks is the round trunk which is a little wider at the base and gradually tapers toward the top as does a bamboo shoot. The split-trunk is also favored for its areas of bare, bleached wood similar in appearance to driftwood. These weathered looking areas, often seen, for example, in juniper, are suggestive of venerable age and endurance against the elements. Coarse bark is also prized for the character it adds to the bonsai.

Yaku-eda and *Imi-eda*

Branches play an important role in bonsai. The essential branches, which give the composition its basic form, are called *yaku-eda*. Awkward or undesirable branches are called *imi-eda*.

(1) *Yaku-eda*

Ichi-no-eda (first branch): The branch closest to the base of the tree, regardless of its size or direction, is called *ichi-no-eda*. The second lowest is *ni-no-eda*, and the third, *san-no-eda* and so on.

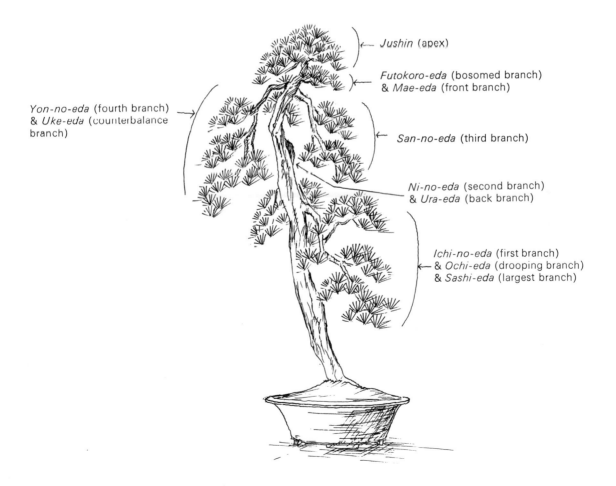

Jushin (apex)

Futokoro-eda (bosomed branch) & *Mae-eda* (front branch)

Yon-no-eda (fourth branch) & *Uke-eda* (counterbalance branch)

San-no-eda (third branch)

Ni-no-eda (second branch) & *Ura-eda* (back branch)

Ichi-no-eda (first branch) & *Ochi-eda* (drooping branch) & *Sashi-eda* (largest branch)

Sashi-eda (largest branch): The largest branch is called *sashi-eda*, and is the most important branch in composing the bonsai style.

Uke-eda (counterbalance branch): The branch extending in the opposite direction of the *sashi-eda* is called the *uke-eda*. It provides visual balance for the *sashi-eda*.

Mae-eda (front branch) & *ura-eda* (back branch): The branches extending toward the front or back are called *mae-eda* or *ura-eda* respectively. They add a sense of depth to the structure.

Futokoro-eda (bosomed branch): A branch that grows between large branches.

Ochi-eda (drooping branch): A branch that droops gracefully downward, "weeping" as a willow. This imparts a tasteful note to the bonsai.

(2)   *Imi-eda*

Kuruma-eda (spoke-like branches): Branches that shoot out from one part of the tree in a radial fashion like spokes of a wheel.

Kannuki-eda (bar branches): Branches extending horizontally to the left and right or to the front and rear.

Kasanari-eda (overlapping branches): Branches that grow at close intervals, extending one above the other, in the same direction.

Tsukidashi-eda (jutting branch): A branch jutting out directly in front.

Hara-eda (belly branch): A branch that protrudes from the inner side of a curve in the trunk.

Sakasa-eda (opposing branch): A branch growing in the opposite direction.

Before Pruning

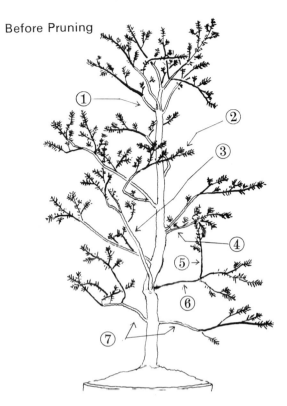

After Pruning

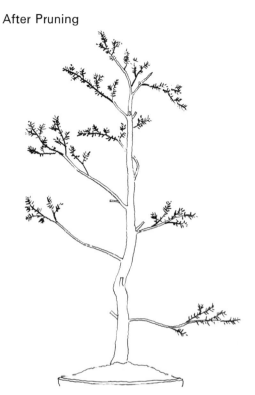

From above

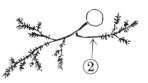

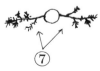

①*Kuruma-eda* (spoke-like branches)
②*Sakasa-eda* (opposing branch)
③*Mae-eda* (front branch)
④*Kasanari-eda* (overlapping branches)
⑤*Tachi-eda* (standing branch)
⑥*Hara-eda* (belly branch)
⑦*Kannuki-eda* (bar branches)

4. Plants Suitable for Bonsai

The kinds of plants suitable for bonsai are roughly specified as follows:

```
┌─Coniferous Bonsai─────────── Needle-leaf trees like pine and Japanese cedar

├─Miscellaneous Bonsai─────┬─ Foliage trees
│                          │
│                          ├─ Broad-leafed trees such as keyaki (sawleaf
│                          │   zelkova) and buna (Japanese beech)
│                          │
│                          ├─ Flowering trees or shrubs such as ume
│                          │   (Japanese flowering apricot) and azalea
│                          │
│                          ├─ Fruit trees
│                          └─ Trees such as Japanese persimmon or orange
│                              which bear fruit or berries
│
└─Herb Bonsai─────────────── Grasses and herbs found in the wild.
```

Some plants do not respond well to the restricted growing conditions of bonsai. The following attributes may be helpful to keep in mind when selecting a plant for bonsai cultivation.

The plant should: (a) be able to be stunted
                        (b) have an ample growth of small leaves
                        (c) have thick twigs and pleasing bark

Many types of plants have already been cultivated as bonsai, but there are others with good potential. The choice is seemingly endless with the great variety of plants growing all over the world in different climates and environmental conditions. It is well worth trying to grow as bonsai, the plants found in your own area.

5. Raising Bonsai

There are many ways of growing young plants for bonsai. The following six methods are the most popular.

1. Collecting wild seedlings
2. Raising from seed
3. Cutting
4. Layering
5. Grafting
6. Dividing roots

Collecting Wild Seedlings

Starting bonsai from seedlings you have sown can save much time and effort. However, wild seedlings possess distinctive qualities that artificially grown plants do not have. Surviving the rigors of wind and snow gives these hardy seedlings character. Such naturally dwarfed plants can be made into a good bonsai within a few year's time, if cultured with due care. Indeed, most bonsai of historical interest have been grown from wild seedlings.

Seedlings Appropriate for Bonsai

Any kind of plant is suitable as long as it can be transplanted and looks attractive in a pot. The following points may be useful to consider before setting out on a collecting expedition.

The plant should be rather small and should also have good root development, small, compact foliage, and an interesting shape as a whole. Dig up only those specimens which show high vitality and promise for future growth.

Looking for Plants in Your Own Neighborhood

Plants with a unique or unusual shape are attractive to beginners, but it is best to avoid such plants. Concentrate instead on familiar seedlings from your own neighborhood. These are easier to raise as bonsai because you can grow them under conditions to which they are already accustomed and subsequently reduce the risk of failure.

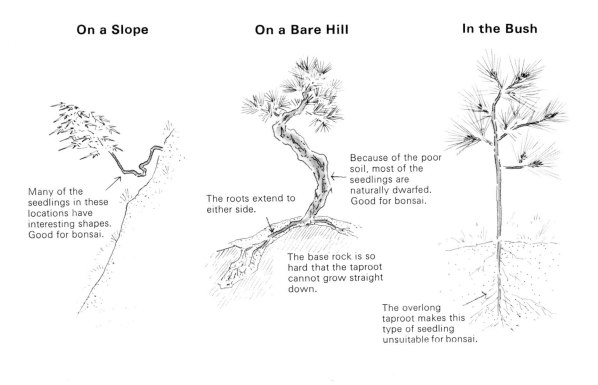

On a Slope

Many of the seedlings in these locations have interesting shapes. Good for bonsai.

On a Bare Hill

The roots extend to either side.

Because of the poor soil, most of the seedlings are naturally dwarfed. Good for bonsai.

The base rock is so hard that the taproot cannot grow straight down.

In the Bush

The overlong taproot makes this type of seedling unsuitable for bonsai.

Equipment for Collecting Wild Seedlings

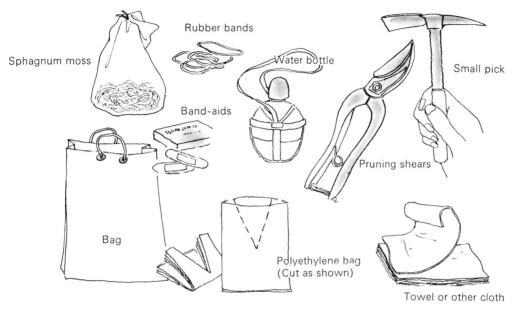

Sphagnum moss

Rubber bands

Water bottle

Small pick

Band-aids

Pruning shears

Bag

Polyethylene bag
(Cut as shown)

Towel or other cloth

Gathering Seedlings

The best season for collecting plants in the wild is early spring, when new buds begin to put forth. As the roots are still dormant, you can safely cut them and dig up the seedling without causing serious injury to the plant. If the seedlings are extremely small, you may dig them up at any time of the year except mid-summer. Those collected in the autumn will require special attention to protect them from the cold.

Methods:

1. When you come across a suitable plant, remove shrubs and grasses growing around it.
2. Prune the leaves and branches that are unnecessary and will interfer with transporting the plant. Unnecessary elements are defined as those which you are certain will not be of use later in shaping the tree.
3. Draw a circle on the ground around the tree. The diameter should be roughly 1/3 the height of the tree. From this circle dig down and then inward toward the tree.

4. In the course of digging, cut the thick roots with a saw, and let thin roots remain intact.
5. Lift the seedling out of the ground making sure to include a good sized ball of soil around the roots so that the hair-roots will not dry out.
6. Wrap the roots with watered sphagnum moss or wet newspapers and tie them up with string. Cover the wrapping with polyethylene sheeting, and secure it tightly with string.

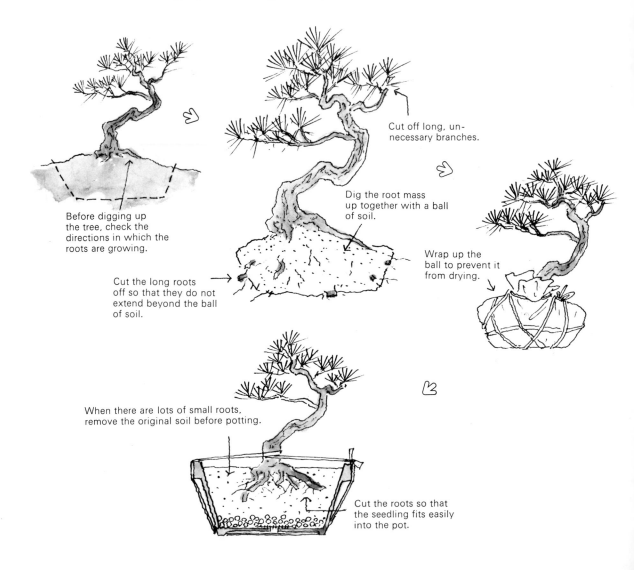

Before digging up the tree, check the directions in which the roots are growing.

Cut the long roots off so that they do not extend beyond the ball of soil.

Cut off long, un-necessary branches.

Dig the root mass up together with a ball of soil.

Wrap up the ball to prevent it from drying.

When there are lots of small roots, remove the original soil before potting.

Cut the roots so that the seedling fits easily into the pot.

Tips for Rooting

1. As soon as you get the plant home, upwrap the sheeting and remove all the soil from the roots.
2. Cut the thick roots with a sharp knife so that they will fit into the container. The cut ends should face downward.
3. Cover the bottom of a wooden box or an unglazed pot with coarse soil, and place the plant in the center. The coarse soil ensures good drainage.
4. Put in main soil and pack it firmly around the roots. Finally, tie the base of the trunk to the container with straw ropes so that the plant is secure in it.

Care After Potting

When the potting process is completed water the plant thoroughly with a fine spray can. By waving the can up and down a rain-like sprinkling can be obtained which reaches all the areas of the plant. Place the plant in a partially shaded area for a week. While the foliage and most of the trunk should be protected from direct sunlight, the base of the trunk should receive enough sun to warm the roots.

A regular watering routine can be established by watching the soil. When the top soil becomes about 70% dry the plant requires water. Eventually you will be able to anticipate when to water, but as a plant's needs for moisture vary with the season, it is best to check the soil initially. It is also important to keep the foliage of the newly potted plant moist.

Once the new buds appear, gradually expose the whole plant to sunlight. It can be set out in the sun for longer periods of time each day until it adapts to the increased levels of light. Nourishment is unnecessary until the plant is well rooted. If potted in spring, it is sufficient to fertilize it once in autumn.

In winter a plant must be protected from the cold. Starting in the spring following the potting and for the next one to two years, the plant must be given sufficient water and fertilizer so that it can continue to gain strength.

Raising Bonsai from Seed

The method of growing bonsai from seed is called *Mishō*. Although this process takes more time than other types of bonsai cultivation, it gives the grower greater control over the plant's development.

Collection and Storage of Seeds

Seeds can be collected in the wild or ordered from nurseries. Those gathered from fields or moutains should be washed to remove any traces of soil or other material. Autumn is the best season for collecting seeds. For storage the seeds may be placed in a plastic bag filled with a mixture of sand and peat moss. The bag should be kept in a cool, dark place. A refrigerator will serve this purpose for certain types of seeds.

When to Sow the Seeds

The best time to sow the seeds is immediately after collecting them. Seeds can also be safely sown in early spring before the budding season.

Preparations for Sowing

Soak the seeds in water overnight. Then place them in a bowl of water and remove any seeds which float to the top, as these will not sprout.

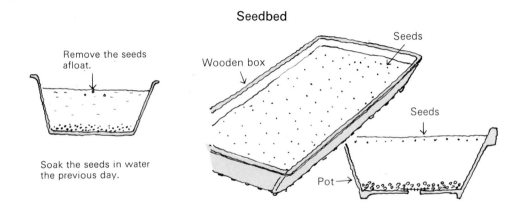

Seedbed

Remove the seeds afloat.

Soak the seeds in water the previous day.

Wooden box

Seeds

Seeds

Pot →

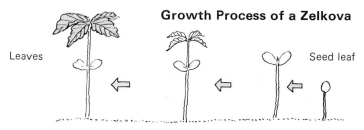

Growth Process of a Zelkova

Leaves · Seed leaf

Seedbed

Use a wooden box or pot for the seedbed. Cover drainage holes with a porous material such as vinyl mesh and secure with wire if necessary. Fill the pot to one quarter of its depth with coarse bottom soil. Then add sieved or a finer grade soil up to approximately 1 cm ($\frac{1}{2}''$) from the top of the pot.

Sowing the seeds

Plant the seeds individually at 3 cm ($1\frac{1}{2}''$) intervals then cover with about 1 cm ($\frac{1}{2}''$) of fine soil. Water thoroughly either with a fine spray from a sprinkling can or by letting water soak from the bottom of the pot upwards to the surface of the soil. The pot is placed in a container filled with water. The water level should equal the level of the soil inside the pot. This method prevents the fine topsoil from being washed away. Protect the newly sown seeds from frost.

Care After Sowing

When there are signs of germination place the pot outdoors in a sunny area. Water the seedlings when the surface of the soil becomes dry and weed as needed. When the seedlings are about three months old a little fertilizer may be applied to the seedbed. Provide adequate frost protection during the cold weather.

Repotting and Continuing Care

Although most deciduous seedlings can be repotted after about six months, pine seedlings should be nearly a year old before repotting. Seedlings should be repotted individually in the springtime shortly before the budding season. Continue the normal cycle of seasonal care so that the plants become well established and ready for their eventual training.

Raising Bonsai from Cuttings

This is a propagation technique, in which a portion of a branch or stem of a plant is cut off and cultivated. Since the cutting is taken from the parent tree, this method is suitable for growing a bonsai which has the same characteristics as its parent. Although this method is not successful with pines, most other trees can be grown from cuttings.

The Cutting Season

Broad-leafed deciduous trees: Cuttings may be taken between February and March from branches grown in the previous year. Cuttings from branches of the current year should be taken between June and September.

Broad-leafed evergreens: June is the best season to take cuttings, when the new branches are well developed.

Needle-leafed evergreens: From the branches of the previous year, take cuttings between April and early May. For cuttings from branches of the current year, the period from July to September is best.

Selecting Cuttings

Choose young branches from a vigorous and healthy plant, as older branches are difficult to root and propagate. When creating a multiple trunk bonsai, select branches which have forked areas.

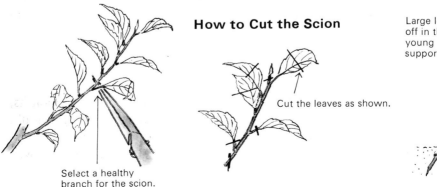

How to Cut the Scion

Select a healthy branch for the scion.

Cut the leaves as shown.

Large leaves should be cut off in the middle, as the young roots can not yet support their growth.

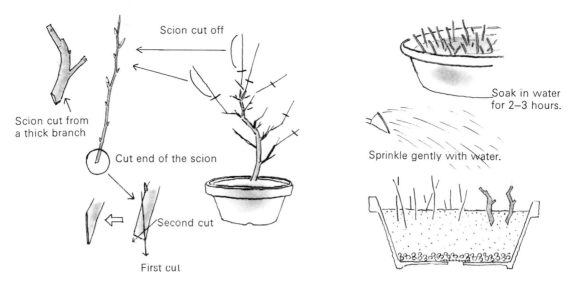

Scion cut off

Scion cut from a thick branch

Cut end of the scion

Second cut

First cut

Soak in water for 2–3 hours.

Sprinkle gently with water.

Preparing the Bed

Use a wooden box or unglazed pot. Cover the bottom third of the container with a layer of coarse soil to ensure good drainage. Then add finer soil until the pot is filled.

Planting

So as not to injure the end of the cuttings, use a stick to make small holes in the soil where the plants will be inserted. Tweezers may be used to position the cuttings. The stems should be put into the soil at a slight angle and sufficient space provided so that the leaves of the various cuttings do not touch each other.

Care After Planting

After the cuttings are planted, water them thoroughly with a watering can and place them under shelter to protect them from wind. As with seedlings, until the roots form, water whenever the soil becomes dry. When the new buds appear—usually within a month—move the container outdoors, gradually lengthening the time of exposure to sunlight. Fertilizer is not necessary for one year, but in winter care should be taken to protect the cuttings from frost.

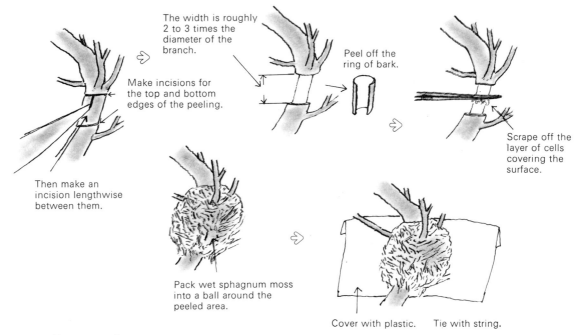

The width is roughly 2 to 3 times the diameter of the branch.

Make incisions for the top and bottom edges of the peeling.

Peel off the ring of bark.

Then make an incision lengthwise between them.

Scrape off the layer of cells covering the surface.

Pack wet sphagnum moss into a ball around the peeled area.

Cover with plastic.   Tie with string.

Layering

Layering is another method of propagation. It allows you to grow roots on a branch that you would like to make into a bonsai, while the branch is still part of the parent plant. The bark of the parent plant is injured to force the growth of new roots. The desired branch with its new roots is then detached and cultivated. Though not suitable for all types of plants, layering offers the advantage of a mature, well established structure from which to start your bonsai.

The Season for Layering

The best time for layering is in the early summer when the branches of the current year are well established. Warm temperatures of 20°C (68°F) and up also help encourage the new roots.

Branches or sections of trunk layered at this time will be ready to detach from the parent tree in the autumn. If layering a main branch or if the layered section is slow to develop roots, one should wait until the following year before separating the new plant from its parent.

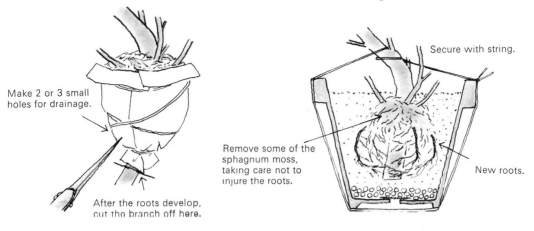

After cutting, set into a pot.

Make 2 or 3 small
holes for drainage.

After the roots develop,
cut the branch off here.

Secure with string.

Remove some of the
sphagnum moss,
taking care not to
injure the roots.

New roots.

Layering Method

Peel off a ring of bark at the section of the parent tree where you intend for the new roots to form. The width of the peeling should be roughly 2 to 3 times the diameter of the layered section. The bark should be removed to a depth that just reaches the woody part of the branch. Pack wet sphagnum moss into a ball around the peeled area, cover it with plastic and tie loosely with string to allow room for watering. If you are not using sphagnum moss, fix a vinyl pot containing fine soil to the peeled area.

Watering

Keep the rooting area moist with regular waterings.

Detaching the Layered Section

Detach layered part from the parent tree when at least ten new roots have sprouted. Trim overgrown branches, if any, and plant the section in a pot. Using string secure the new plant in the pot to protect it against wind, as the roots are still too delicate and sparse to fully support the plant.

Grafting

Grafting is a method for joining two plants of the same genus. The branch or shoot to be grafted is called the "scion" and the tree which receives it is called the "stock." Often the scion will be cultivated and the stock an uncultivated or wild variety of the same species.

By grafting, the characteristics of the scion are completely transferred to the root stock. Moreover, this method can be used to accelerate the production of fruit or flowers. Grafting is frequently used for floral or fruit bearing bonsai. However, it is a technique that requires skill and experience.

The Grafting Season

The dormant season from December to February is appropriate for grafting.

Cutting the Scion

Choose as your scion a year old branch from a healthy, vigorous tree. Cut from the parent plant during the dormant season. After cutting is completed wrap the scion in agricultural plastic and keep buried in the ground at a depth of about 30—50 cm (approx. 12—20″) or keep refrigerated at 10—5°C (34°—41°F) until ready for use.

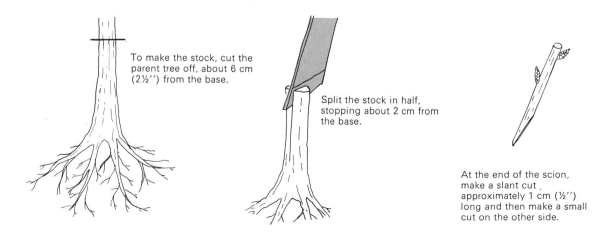

To make the stock, cut the parent tree off, about 6 cm (2½″) from the base.

Split the stock in half, stopping about 2 cm from the base.

At the end of the scion, make a slant cut approximately 1 cm (½″) long and then make a small cut on the other side.

Selecting the Stock

Stock should be similar in kind to the scion or of a kindred species. It must be a plant with dense roots. Choose stock with a diameter nearly equal that of the scion or else an unsightly gap may occur at the grafting junction.

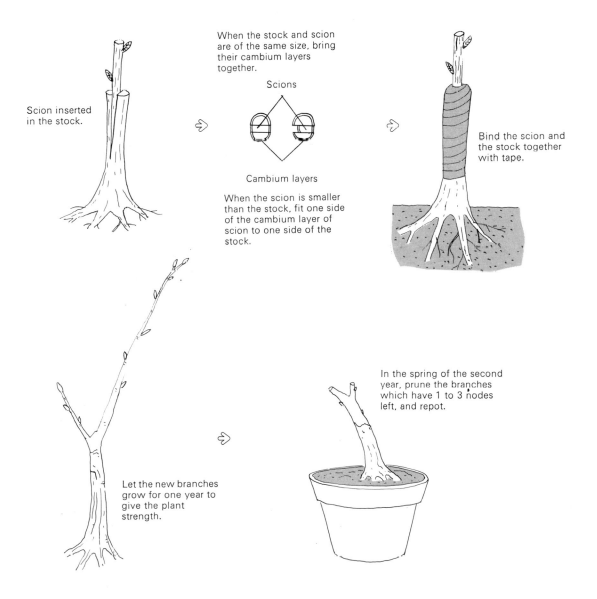

Scion inserted in the stock.

When the stock and scion are of the same size, bring their cambium layers together.

Scions

Cambium layers

When the scion is smaller than the stock, fit one side of the cambium layer of scion to one side of the stock.

Bind the scion and the stock together with tape.

Let the new branches grow for one year to give the plant strength.

In the spring of the second year, prune the branches which have 1 to 3 nodes left, and repot.

Dividing

Dividing is a means of propagation by which the root mass is divided into several sections. It is most suited to herbs of the perennial family or shrubs. The divided plant has the same characteristics as its parent. Moreover, quick root formation is assured and there is less danger of seriously harming the plant than with some of the other propagation methods.

Using this method with well established shrubs gives you a head start in enjoying the shape of your bonsai as the form will have been previously developed as part of the original single plant.

The Dividing Season

The best time for dividing is just before the new buds begin to swell or in the autumn after the leaves have fallen.

Dividing the Roots

In applying this method to foliage plants, dig up the root mass and separate into appropriate sizes with hands or scissors, pluck off any rotten roots or leaves and then plant the sections individually. With shrubs, separate joined sections of the roots or stock with scissors or a saw, if necessary. Before potting, the rough surface of the cutting should be smoothed with a sharp knife.

Trees

Flowering quince

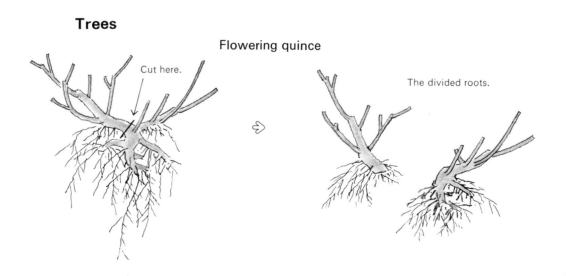

Cut here.

The divided roots.

Care After Transplating

After transplanting, water the plant thoroughly from above. The pot should be placed in a sunny area where it is not too windy. Water the plant whenever the surface of the soil is dry and give normal, year-round care.

Bulbous Plants

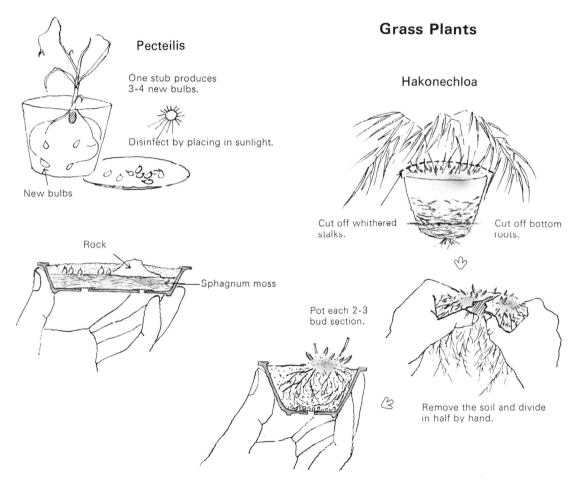

Pecteilis

One stub produces 3-4 new bulbs.

Disinfect by placing in sunlight.

New bulbs

Rock

Sphagnum moss

Grass Plants

Hakonechloa

Cut off whithered stalks.

Cut off bottom roots.

Pot each 2-3 bud section.

Remove the soil and divide in half by hand.

6. Care of Bonsai

Equipment necessary for repotting

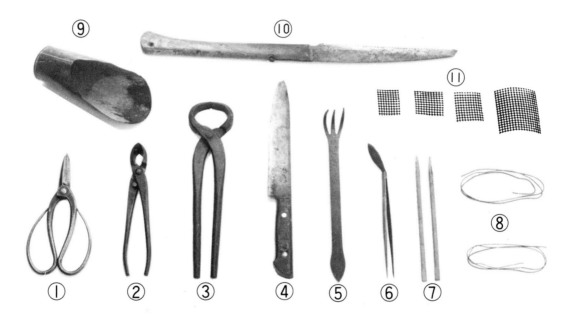

①Scissors for cutting roots ②−③Pincers for cutting thick roots ④Knife for cutting roots inside the pot ⑤Rake for disentangling roots ⑥Tweezers for arranging roots ⑦Bamboo chopsticks for disentangling roots and arranging the soil in the pot ⑧Wire for securing plants ⑨Shovel for filling the pot with soil ⑩Saw for cutting thick roots ⑪Wire mesh for covering drainage holes in the pot

Tools and Equipment

Various bonsai tools and equipment are available but not all of them are essential for starting bonsai. Initially, a pair of scissors or other tools that you already own may be adequate. As your skill develops, however, it may seem more convenient and efficient to use some specialized bonsai equipment for your operations.

The photo shows basic tools and equipment for performing most ordinary bonsai functions.

Repotting

Why is repotting necessary? As bonsai growth is restricted by a limited space, it is natural that in time the pot will become too confining. If the plant is not repotted, existing roots would become unhealthily crowded and there would be no room for new root development.

Soil replacement is also a very important part of repotting. In addition to water and nourishment, the roots also obtain air through the soil. Thus, the soil must be in good condition to properly aid the plant in respiration and provide the necessary nutrients.

A plant left potted in the same soil for many years can loose its vitality. Coarse soil may break into fragments from weathering or from uncontrolled root growth and eventually these fragments harden into a mass which hinders the passage of water and air. This causes malnutrition and dangerous weakening of the plant.

Repotting quickens the plant's metabolism. The attendant soil replacement promotes good drainage and aeration and provides an opportunity for necessary root trimming which stimulates new growth.

The Repotting Season

The best time for repotting is just before the budding season when trees awake from their dormant state. During this period, the roots recover quickly from pruning.

Before Repotting

This needle juniper was repotted four years ago. The roots, due to substantial growth during this period, have pushed their way through the surface. This indicates a need for repotting.

Lift the Trunk out of the Pot

If the tree can not be dislodged, cut the roots around the edge of the pot.

Disentangle the Roots

With bamboo chopsticks, disentagle the roots, starting from the side and then working towards the bottom.

Prune the Roots

Prune the disentagled roots with sharp scissors, taking care not to crush the cut ends.

Check Carefully

Pick out eggs and larvae of pests if any. Remove grassroots or weeds.

Preparing the Pot

Cover the holes with wire mesh. Run two wires through the holes. These will be used to secure the plant in the pot. Cover the bottom with coarse soil.

Settle the Plant

Place the plant in the desired position within the pot. If necessary, trim more roots on the bottom.

Secure the Plant

Move the trunk around right and left so that it settles firmly, then tie it and the roots in place with the wires.

Put in the Soil

Put in the soil and spread it with bamboo chopsticks so that it is evenly distributed. Tap the edge of the pot to make the soil settle firmly.

Brush the Surface

When the pot is filled with soil, level the surface with a brush. Remove excess soil.

Press with a Trowel

Cover the surface with fine soil, and press it with a trowel from the edge of the pot toward the center.

The Repotting Process Completed

To complete the repotting process, water the soil sufficiently with a sprinkling can. Take care that the water does not wash away the top soil.

How Often to Repot

The frequency of repotting depends upon the type of tree, its health, the size of the pot, and the kind of soil, etc. Principally, repotting should be done when it becomes difficult for water and air to penetrate the soil. You can discern the need for repotting when water sprinkled over the soil is not absorbed smoothly or remains puddled on the soil's surface.

Repotting Frequency According to Tree Type

Conifer: Young trees that are in training require repotting once every two to three years. Well established trees require it only once every three to five years.

Deciduous Trees: Young deciduous trees that are in training require repotting once a year. More mature deciduous trees, i.e., those with established shapes, need repotting only once every one to two years.

Soils

Because bonsai trees are grown in soil that is prepared by the trainer, the selection of soils is very important. It is essential that bonsai soils be air permeable and provide good drainage. The soils should also be suited to the climate where the bonsai will be raised and should be easy to acquire.

Each soil has distinctive features: Coarse reddish soil retains moisture well and provides noursihment. Smooth, hard, sand-like soil is air permeable and drains well, but tends to dry out faster and is low in nourishment.

The advantages of both types of soil can be enjoyed by using a combination of the two. A greater proportion of sand-like soil is preferred in rainy climates or for use by bonsai growers who are able to water their plants several times a day. Greater quantities of reddish soil in the mixture are preferred by persons having less time for watering or in cases where bonsai are set in airy, open places. Thus, the proportion of soils in the mixture is based on the bonsai's environment and upon the kind of care it will receive.

Placement

Sunshine and air are important

Be sure to place the bonsai where it can receive plenty of sunlight and fresh air. This is essential for the health of the tree because the sun and the air contain nutritive elements. These elements are absorbed through the leaves in a process known as assimilation.

Light breezes which circulate through the plant's foliage and branches enrich the young shoots. A sunny, airy setting also helps keep the plant free from excess moisture and insect damage.

Placement during the summer

The foliage of certain trees—those with small, densely packed leaves such as silver fir (yezo spruce), Japanese hemlock, or cedar—can sometimes become sunburned. Under the strong summer sun the amount of water absorbed from the roots may not be sufficient to cover the amount of moisture evaporated from the leaves. Sunburned leaves hinder the normal growth of the plant and reduce the chance of colorful autumn foliage.

Trees of the previously mentioned types must be protected from over exposure to intense summer rays. Avoid a western exposure which is particularly strong and hang reed screens or cheesecloth over the shelves where the bonsai are kept.

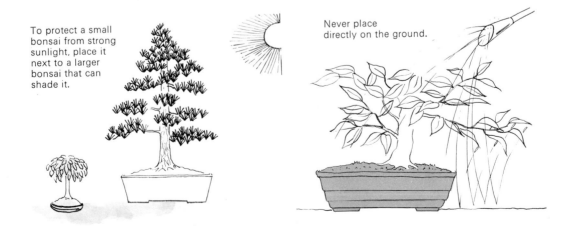

To protect a small bonsai from strong sunlight, place it next to a larger bonsai that can shade it.

Never place directly on the ground.

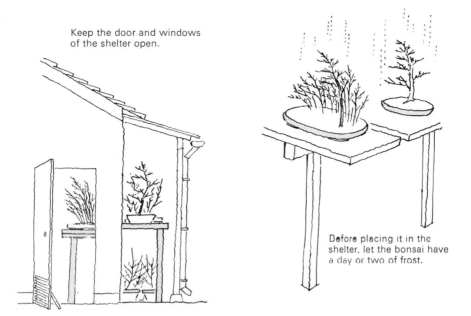

Keep the door and windows of the shelter open.

Before placing it in the shelter, let the bonsai have a day or two of frost.

Placement during the winter

Winter care differs according to the climate in which the bonsai is raised. In areas which experience severe winters with temperatures constantly below the freezing point and/or heavy snows, the bonsai should be protected. A day or two of light frost, however, will not harm the plant.

There is little danger of damage from the cold in relatively mild climates. Here the main concern would be overexposure to the wind and frost. Left completely open to the wind, leaves and branches may die from a loss of moisture.

Protection may take the form of a coldframe or shelter covered on top and three sides with laths or straw matting. The south side of the shelter is the one usually left open. An alternative to this in fairly mild climates is to place the bonsai under the eaves of a roof.

Bonsai which are hardy do not have to be brought into the shelter too hastily. They may be exposed to frost two or three times before winter protection starts. The frost is actually a signal which informs the plant of the approaching dormant season. Without a sufficient period of dormancy, the plant may grow or bud prematurely. This could weaken it and lead to poor flower bearing.

In early spring the bonsai should be removed from the shelter. It is important to bring the plant out at the first sign of germination and not later. If the buds are allowed to fully develop while the plant is still inside, when it is brought out even a slight cold spell could injure the sensitive buds and interfere with normal growth. Partial protection such as placing the plant under eaves is helpful in letting the plant adjust gradually to the remaining chill.

Placement of the Bonsai Pot

(1) Never place the pot directly on the ground where mud can form during rains or watering. Mud soils the leaves and container and is unhealthy for the plant. Bonsai placed on the ground are also susceptible to earthworms, ants or slugs, which may creep up through the pot's drainage holes.

(2) The bonsai pot should be turned around occasionally so that all sides of the plant can benefit equally from sunlight and air circulation. Turning the plant also helps maintain balance in the development of branches and foliage.

(3) Bonsai are truly outdoor plants. They will weaken if kept in a house for several days. The humidity in heated or air cooled rooms is too low for bonsai. If a plant is displayed indoors for a special occasion it should not be left in a room for more than a day or two. To keep the plant healthy at such times expose it to two or three hours of fresh air per day and sprinkle the foliage with water.

Watering

Water when the surface of the soil gets dry. Water the plant thoroughly from above until the soil is saturated and water begins to drip from the drainage hole at the bottom. Because bonsai are living things there are some differences even among plants of the same type, bred under the same conditions. Thus, the rate of water absorption may vary with each plant. As a result, there may be no exact schedule for watering. The best bet is to observe carefully and water when needed.

The relation between roots and water

The root develops seeking the water necessary for its survival. If the soil in the pot is constantly moist, the root may not continue to develop, thus endangering the plant's vitality. In addition, the root absorbs oxygen through respiration. Soil which is constantly moist from overwatering can cause fatal oxygen starvation in the plant.

For these reasons overwatering is as much a danger to the plant's health as insufficient watering. Be sure never to water soil that is still moist.

Watering on rainy days

During rainy periods when the bonsai soil becomes wet it may seem that watering is unnecessary. However, it is often the case that the rainfall moistens only the surface and does not actually saturate the rest of the soil. Special care must be taken—particularly with densely foliaged trees—to ensure that the soil is thoroughly moistened. Check the bottom of the pot and if it is dry, additional watering is needed.

When a prolonged rain causes a build-up of water in the pot place a stone or small piece of wood under one side so that the pot is tilted and can drain more quickly.

During the winter plants should be watered on relatively warm days in the morning.

A small bonsai placed in a corner is liable to be overlooked when watering. Be sure to place a smaller one before a larger one so that none will be overlooked.

It takes time for water to soak into the soil. Watering twice at an interval of about five minutes will ensure the plant a sufficient amount of water.

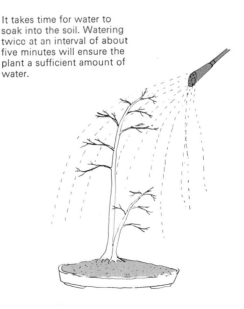

Fertilizer

Fertilizer can be broadly divided into two categories: organic such as soybean or cottonseed meal and inorganic such as chemical fertilizer.

The advantage of chemical fertilizer is that plants respond quickly to it with new growth. The fertilizer is potent and rapidly releases its nutrients. A very small amount of chemical fertilizer is sufficient and care must be taken not to give an overlarge dose. An excessive amount is too rich for the plant and may cause its death.

Organic fertilizers are slower to take effect. They are often mixed with the potting soil or are dissolved in water and then applied. Though not as fast acting as artificial fertilizers, organic fertilizers are safer as they release nutrients slowly over a longer period of time. Consequently there is less danger of harming the plant through overfeeding.

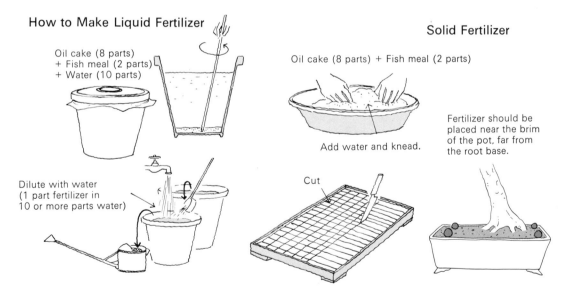

How to Make Liquid Fertilizer

Oil cake (8 parts)
+ Fish meal (2 parts)
+ Water (10 parts)

Dilute with water
(1 part fertilizer in
10 or more parts water)

Solid Fertilizer

Oil cake (8 parts) + Fish meal (2 parts)

Add water and knead.

Cut

Fertilizer should be
placed near the brim
of the pot, far from
the root base.

Feeding

Feeding differs according to the age of the bonsai. For younger trees still being trained, fertilizer should be applied in early spring as the plant awakes from the dormant season. This encourages the growth of new buds and branches.

Mature trees with well established branches do not require extra nourishment in the spring. Because fertilizer applied in the growing season forces branches to widen or foliage to grow more thickly, trees which have already attained the desired form should not be fed then. An autumn feeding is preferable as it will not produce new growth, which could interfere with the tree's shape.

Also, fertilizer should not be given to a tree in poor condition during mid-summer or after a long rain as the roots are not strong enough at those times to absorb nutrition.

When to Repot

Repotting after a long rain, or in mid-summer should be avoided. The roots are not able to absorb nutrition immediately after repotting because they have been trimmed. Fertilizer may be applied one month after repotting. By this time the damaged roots will have started to recover and the new roots will have extended.

Pests

As bonsai are living plants they are sometimes subject to disease or pests. When there are signs of damage or infestation, treatment should be given immediately. Even a day or two of delay can cause additional injury to the plant.

Insecticides are effective even if rain falls on the plant as little as two hours after treatment, so there is no need to delay even in the advent of bad weather. Fast action is the best policy.

Protective Care

Although in times of emergency a quick response is best, better still is conscientious protective care for your bonsai.

Make sure that basic care is adequate by keeping pace with the plant's need for water, nourishment, air, and space for the roots to grow without jamming.

Check frequently to see that the plant remains hardy. Plants which are weak, diseased, or placed in poorly ventilated areas are more susceptible to pests.

Spray the plant with insecticide twice a month from before the active season in early spring until the dormant period in the fall.

7. Training Bonsai

The appreciation of bonsai takes a different form from the appreciation of other plants. Potted plants, for example, may be considered beautiful in terms of particular features such as lovely flowers or well shaped leaves. With bonsai the total aesthetic effect of the plant is the most important thing. Leaves, trunk, and roots while individually attractive must also work as harmonious elements of the entire composition.

The process of working with the plant to achieve the desired form is called training. Training involves several techniques, all of which help the plant attain pleasing proportions. Some of these techniques are discussed in the following paragraphs.

Pinching Buds

Bud pinching is a method of controlling new growth. How and when to remove the buds depends on the type of tree. The condition and location of the buds should also be considered in deciding which ones to pinch. Buds which are located in places where new growth is desired should be left to develop. Others should be removed. Where several buds appear at one spot such as with pines, pinch off one or two buds at their mid-points and cut the others off from the base. This can be done with fingers or shears. Buds which are too large or too small should be pinched off leaving only those which are middle sized. The appropriate time for pinching is in the spring while the buds are still soft and have barely begun to put forth needles.

With other types of trees new buds tend to appear at the base of branches and roots, places where nourishment intake is heavy. If allowed to remain, these buds will form new growth which would detract from the bonsai's established shape and look of maturity.

Encouraging axillary growth

If the growth of axillary branches is desired, pinch off the terminal buds. The terminal bud produces a hormone that restricts the growth of the side (axillary) buds. Removing the terminal buds means that the side buds may now grow freely and that more sap and nutrients are available to them. This results in accelerated growth for the axillary buds as they develop into branches.

Five-needle Pine

This part grows fast.

Pinch off a little of the weak shoots.

Pinch the strong shoots off short.

Japanese Yew

Middle part

Strong part

Weak part

Leaves of the previous year

New shoots

Clip off about ⅔ of a strong shoot.

Clip off about ½ of a normal shoot

Clip only a third of a weak shoot.

Japanese Cedar

Portion to be pinched off

Hinoki Cypress

When the shoot is strong, pinch off here.

The tip is usually pinched off.

Leaf Cutting

This training method can be used only on healthy trees of species vigorous enough to undergo this type of treatment. The purpose of this training technique is to increase the number of branches and to force a new crop of smaller and more beautiful leaves.

Leaf trimming is performed on deciduous trees such as Japanese maple, zelkova, and sal (saul). The leaves of evergreens must never be cut. Instead, the buds of non-deciduous trees such as Japanese black pine or red pine are pinched off as previously described.

As shown in the illustration the leaves must be thoroughly trimmed starting at the base. This operation should be performed when the current year's foliage has become firmly established.

This method of leaf trimming forces the plant to form new buds twice a year. As this requires much energy, fertilizer should be applied before leaf trimming to strengthen the plant.

Maple

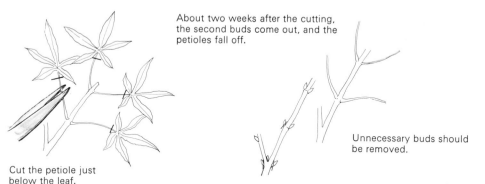

About two weeks after the cutting, the second buds come out, and the petioles fall off.

Cut the petiole just below the leaf.

Unnecessary buds should be removed.

Temperature and budding

Warmer temperatures encourage the germination of buds. Leaf trimming or bud pinching is recommended only for areas where summer temperatures reach at least 25°C (77°F). Under such conditions the tree can respond to these training measures with new growth.

Pruning

Pruning is the term for shortening or cutting off elements of the plant such as the roots and branches. Both the health and the appearance of the tree benefit from pruning. As stated, it helps the shape and visual balance of the tree.

In addition, more sunlight is admitted to essential parts of the bonsai when unwanted growth is eliminated. Short branches growing in the shadow of dense foliage can actually wither from a lack of light. Therefore, pruning is necessary to expose every part of the tree to the sun and to aid in breeding the short branches which figure so importantly in the overall form of the bonsai.

The pruning season

The best time for pruning trunks or big branches is in the early spring just before the buds start to open. Because of the approaching period of active growth, the plant can begin quickly to recover from the pruning.

Deciding which branches to prune

Though as a beginner it may seem hard at first to decide which branches to remove, the choice becomes easier when considering the bonsai's shape as a whole. In addition it is helpful to know about "*imi-eda,*" the unwanted branches of bonsai. *Imi-eda*, a term used throughout bonsai's long history, means the awkward or unsightly branches which detract from the form you are trying to create. A description of *imi-eda* is found on page 36.

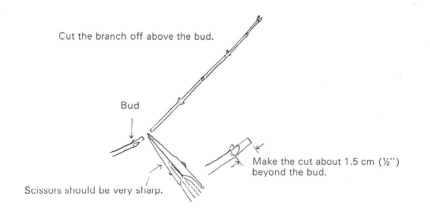

Cut the branch off above the bud.

Bud

Make the cut about 1.5 cm (½″) beyond the bud.

Scissors should be very sharp.

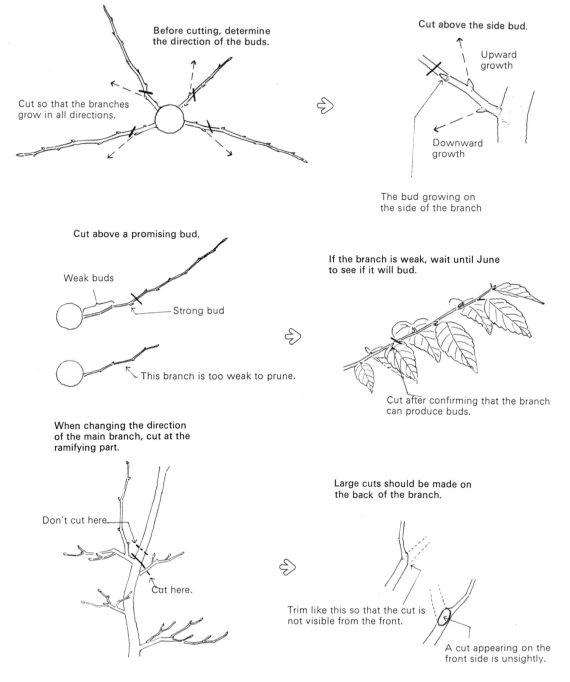

Before cutting, determine the direction of the buds.

Cut so that the branches grow in all directions.

Cut above the side bud.

Upward growth

Downward growth

The bud growing on the side of the branch

Cut above a promising bud.

Weak buds

Strong bud

This branch is too weak to prune.

If the branch is weak, wait until June to see if it will bud.

Cut after confirming that the branch can produce buds.

When changing the direction of the main branch, cut at the ramifying part.

Don't cut here.

Cut here.

Large cuts should be made on the back of the branch.

Trim like this so that the cut is not visible from the front.

A cut appearing on the front side is unsightly.

Wiring

Wiring is a training technique with which trunk and branch defects can be corrected. The part of the tree to be changed is wired into the desired shape or position and left for several months. The wires are removed when the tree has grown into its new form.

Two kinds of wire are used for this method: copper and aluminum. Copper wire should be annealed first in a low temperature fire. It can then be easily bent into shape and wrapped around the trunk or branch. Once used however, it is somewhat difficult to straighten again for reuse on another tree. Because copper wire holds so securely it is most appropriate for coniferous trees, which have comparartively elastic xylem.

For deciduous trees with sensitive, easily marred bark, aluminum wire is recommended. Aluminum wire is softer than copper wire, but does not fasten as securely. Therefore, the wire must be of a thicker gauge in order to control the trunk or branch.

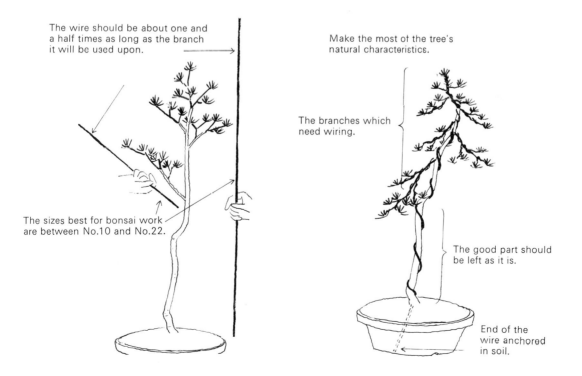

The wire should be about one and a half times as long as the branch it will be used upon.

The sizes best for bonsai work are between No.10 and No.22.

Make the most of the tree's natural characteristics.

The branches which need wiring.

The good part should be left as it is.

End of the wire anchored in soil.

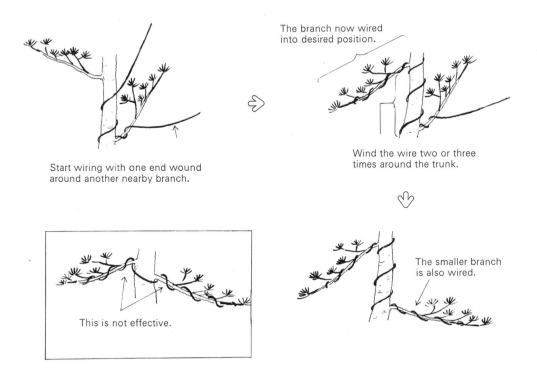

The branch now wired into desired position.

Start wiring with one end wound around another nearby branch.

Wind the wire two or three times around the trunk.

This is not effective.

The smaller branch is also wired.

When to wire

The best season to wire coniferous trees is between September, when plants enter the dormant season, and spring before the buds begin to appear.

Deciduous trees are better wired after the tree awakes from its dormant period. Leaves may be grown to full size but the branches should still be supple. Although the winter's bare branches are easier to see and work with, the early buds are so delicate that even the slightest touch could injure them. For this reason it is safer to wire the tree after the buds have finished developing.

When to remove the wire

Wired bonsai must be kept under constant observation. As the tree grows the wire may become too tight and damage the bark. In this event the wire must be removed immediately. Watching the tree carefully, however, prevents such a situation.

Needle juniper (*Juniperus rigida* Sieb. et Zucc.)
60 years old, 70 cm (2'4''), *Chokkan*

Yesso spruce (*Picea glehnii* Mast.)
120 years old, 60 cm (2'), *Moyogi*

74

Japanese flowering apricot (*Prunus mume* Sieb. et Zucc.)
50 years old, 60 cm (2'), *Moyogi*

Maple (*Acer palmatum* Thunb. var. *matumurae* Makino)
30 years old, 70 cm (2'4''), *Moyogi*

Japanese cedar (*Cryptomeria japonica* D. Don.)
30 years old, 80 cm (2'7''), *Yose-ue*

Columbine
(*Aquilegia akitensis* Huth)

Apple (right)
(*Malus pumila* Mill.
var. *domestica* Schneider)
10 years old,
12 cm (5'') *Moyogi*

Big quaking grass (left)
(*Briza maxima* L.)

Crab-apple (right)
(*Malus micromalus* Makino)
10 years old, 20 cm (8'')
Kengai

Jointweed (left)
(*Polygonum hydropiper* L.)

Garlic
(*Allium Thunbergii* G. Don)

79

English holly (*Ilex serrata* Thunb. var. *sieboldii* Loes.)
30 years old, 70 cm (2'4''), *Kabudachi*

Five-needle pine (*Pinus parviflora* Sieb. et Zucc.)
90 years old, 80 cm (2'7''), *Bankan*

Winter jasmine (*Jasminum nudiflorum* Lindl.)
30 years old, 60 cm (2'), *Ishitsuki*

Five-needle pine (*Pinus parviflora* Sieb. et Zucc.)
50 years old, 80 cm (2'7''), *Sokan*

Needle juniper (*Juniperus rigida* Sieb. et Zucc.)
90 years old, 80 cm (2'7''), *Bunjingi*

8. How to Shape Bonsai Styles

What is most important is to observe the plant carefully from every angle so as to discover its best features. Utilizing them aids in the creation of a striking bonsai. You are, in other words, lending a helping hand to bring out the plant's natural beauty.

The best season to get to work on shaping is spring, just before the buds begin to appear after the long dormant season. There is no danger of injuring the branches by pruning at this time of year, because the plants are so vigorous that they soon recover.

The procedure:
(1) Choose which is to be the front side of the bonsai, keeping in mind the directions in which the roots are growing.
(2) Prune unnecessary twigs and branches.
(3) Adjust the form as desired by wiring and bending.
(4) Repot the bonsai.

Pruning the Branches and Twigs

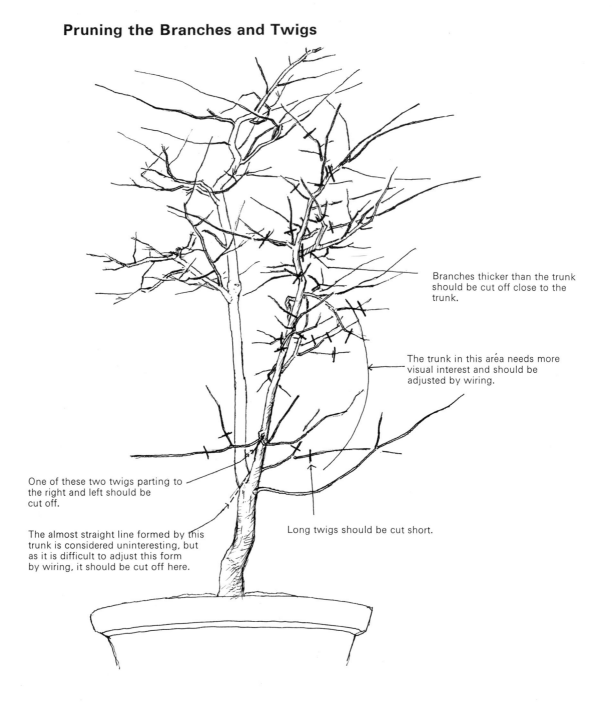

Branches thicker than the trunk should be cut off close to the trunk.

The trunk in this area needs more visual interest and should be adjusted by wiring.

One of these two twigs parting to the right and left should be cut off.

The almost straight line formed by this trunk is considered uninteresting, but as it is difficult to adjust this form by wiring, it should be cut off here.

Long twigs should be cut short.

Deciding upon Root Placement

Strong roots should extend
to the right and left.

Roots Viewed from Above

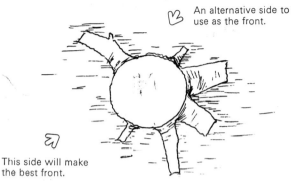

An alternative side to
use as the front.

This side will make
the best front.

Don't place a thick root directly
in front. A visual line leading
to the side of the bonsai is more
graceful.

Trimming the Roots

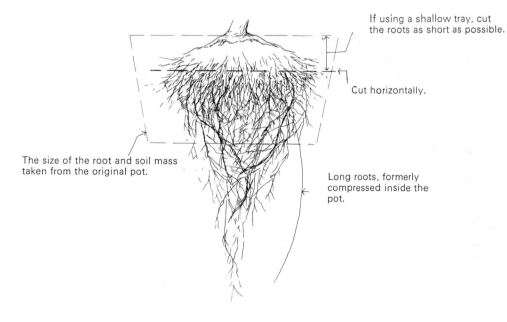

If using a shallow tray, cut
the roots as short as possible.

Cut horizontally.

The size of the root and soil mass
taken from the original pot.

Long roots, formerly
compressed inside the
pot.

Preparing the Pot

Securing the Wire Mesh

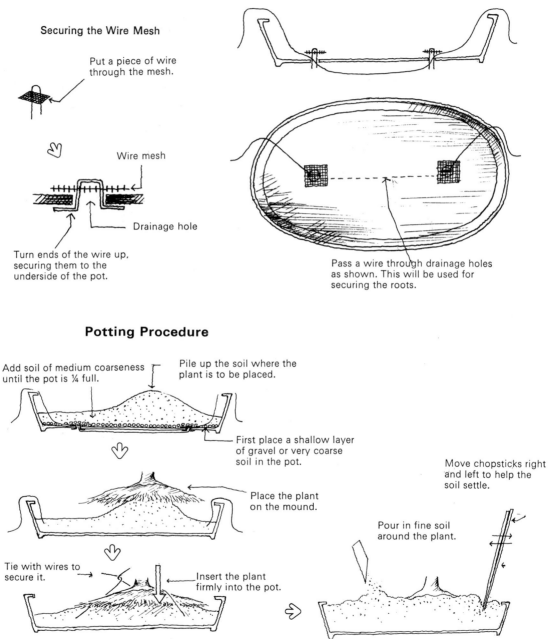

Put a piece of wire through the mesh.

Wire mesh

Drainage hole

Turn ends of the wire up, securing them to the underside of the pot.

Pass a wire through drainage holes as shown. This will be used for securing the roots.

Potting Procedure

Add soil of medium coarseness until the pot is ¼ full.

Pile up the soil where the plant is to be placed.

First place a shallow layer of gravel or very coarse soil in the pot.

Place the plant on the mound.

Tie with wires to secure it.

Insert the plant firmly into the pot.

Move chopsticks right and left to help the soil settle.

Pour in fine soil around the plant.

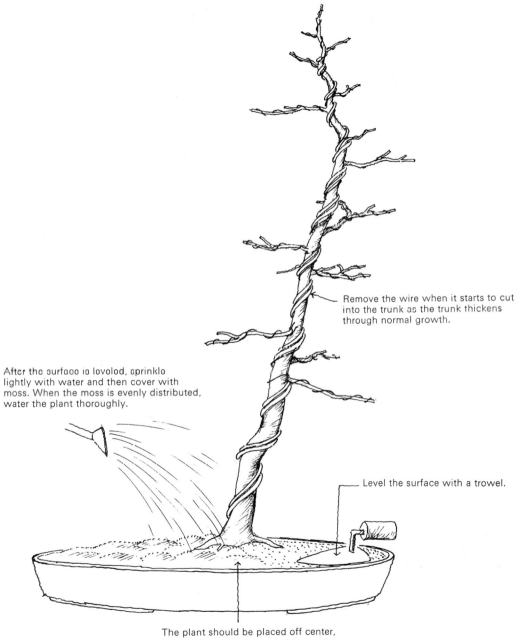

Remove the wire when it starts to cut
into the trunk as the trunk thickens
through normal growth.

After the surface is leveled, sprinkle
lightly with water and then cover with
moss. When the moss is evenly distributed,
water the plant thoroughly.

Level the surface with a trowel.

The plant should be placed off center,
a little to the right or left.

9. Practical Techniques

Single Trunk

13 year old Japanese Black Pine Grown from Seed

When the plant is left alone, the upper part tends to become vigorous and the lower part weak. The photo shows typical example of this.

Conifers have long leaves. Since the old leaves tend to hide the branches, remove leaves more than a year old. When you obtain the desired clear view, study the shape carefully as it is. In the case pictured here, it would be best to make the most of the curve near the base of the trunk by shaping it into a *moyogi* style.

The end of the wire must be firmly fixed.
Push it through the soil until the end
touches the bottom of the pot.

If the tip of the wire is too short to bend
with your fingers, use pliers to wrap it
around the branch.

When you bend a trunk or a branch, make
sure that the wire is wrapped around the
outside of the curve, otherwise·it will be
ineffective.

When you have finished wiring the trunk,
work on the branches and twigs. Let the top
twig stand erect so that it can form the *shin*
or core of the bonsai.

Branches on the inside of
a curve should be removed.

Branches on the outside of
a curve can remain.

The direction of branches of untrained
trees differ according to the stages of
growth. On young trees the branches
grow upward, on mature trees, they
grow horizontally, and finally when
the tree becomes old, the branches
grow downward. This bonsai represents
the mature stage, so the branches
were bent horizontally, which helps
create the illusion of a somewhat
aged tree.

Repot for Display

When the fundamental shape is
formed, repot the plant to a container
for display. Because this is a *moyogi*
style bonsai with a slender trunk, a
round, hand-made pot was selected to
set it off. As the bonsai is already tall
enough, care must be taken to
maintain the present height by
pruning the buds, and allowing the
plant to produce as much foliage as
possible.

Cascade Style

Five Year Old Needle Juniper from a Cutting

Some trees have a tendency to grow sideways. It is not advisable to force them into a standing shape. Instead, take advantage of their characteristics and train them into a cascade style.

Stabilize the Pot

A plant such as this is very likely to be unstable because of its long branches. By placing the whole plant in a larger pot, you can easily stabilize it.

When several branches are growing from the same part of the tree, remove the unnecessary ones.

A drooping crown makes the bonsai look dull. Wire and then raise it with a lever.

The cascade style represents a tree blown by the wind. The twigs, therefore, do not grow upward or downward. Use twigs growing right and left for graceful lateral lines.

Scrape soil off the roots, prune rootlets, and allow the rootage to show above the surface of the soil.

Repot for Display

Use a deep pot so that the contor of gravity may remain firmly in the pot. The plant must be fixed securely with a wire passed through the drainage holes.

The Crown of the Cascade Style

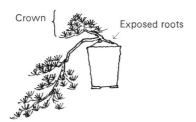

Crown

Exposed roots

Crown

Group Plantings

There are no restrictions on the number of trees to be planted in group, but traditional groupings have always had an odd number. If the number of trees available is less than ten, it is advisable to plant five or seven.

Make the tallest and thickest tree the main one, and plant around it at unequal intervals those which have a variety of heights. This will add depth and width to the bonsai.

One of the most important matters in group plantings is to leave space on one side of the pot rather than to plant the trees all over. This makes the scenery look larger. For beginners a good method is to form the trees into two or three groups and to plant them with the main tree in the center.

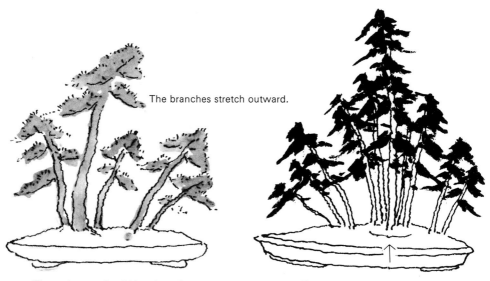

The branches stretch outward.

The main tree should be planted a bit off-center.

If the group of trees around the main tree are of the same species, the entire composition looks well balanced.

Hinoki cypress from cuttings. Saplings grown from the same parent are best for group plantings, since they have similar forms and characteristics.

Before planting, cut and trim the branches of each sapling.

If necessary, correct the form of the trunk by wiring before moving to a new pot.

Cut the bottom roots so that the trees may stand upright on their own.

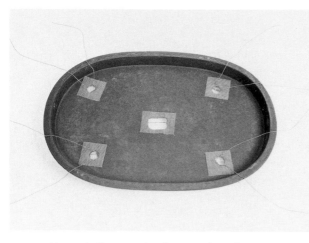

Use a shallow tray for the container. Cover the drainage holes with mesh, and pass wires through for fixing the trees.

To find the most pleasing arrangement for your trees, try them first in various temporary arrangements in the pot. As you work, keep the location of the central tree in mind.

When you have decided upon the positions and fixed them, pour some soil in around the roots and then wiggle the tips of bamboo chopsticks between the roots to settle the soil.

Fix the trees with the wires, which were previously passed through the drainage holes.

Add more soil until the pot is almost full and the wires are hidden. Sweep the surface with a small broom to remove excess soil.

Press the soil all over with a trowel in order to settle it.

Lastly, cover with fine soil and then water the soil well.

If water runs down the trunks and forms a hollow around the bases of the trees, add more soil to rebuild the area.

Rock Plantings

Trees combined with a rock represent natural scenery in a realistic way. There are two basic styles of rock planting. One is to plant the tree in an indented part of the rock, and the other is to let the roots grow over and around the rock and finally reach into the pot. In the latter style, the roots seem to embrace the rock.

Any kind of tree with long, thin roots is suitable for rock planting. The rock should preferably have a rough surface. If smooth, it is hard for the roots to grow. As to the soil, a mixture of peat and about 20% red loam is frequently used.

Japanese Maple (left) and Obsidian found in a river (right)

Cut off thick roots close to the base so that the plant may easily settle on the rock.

Before planting, secure the branches with wire to obtain the desired form.

Determine the best position for the tree with regard to the rock.

Glue the ends of several wires to the underside of the rock with an adhesive agent. The wires are used to secure the plant.

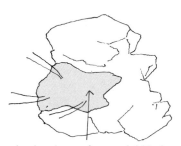

Apply a layer of a special kind of soil, known as peat muck to the spot where the tree is to be planted.

Secure the tree with wire.

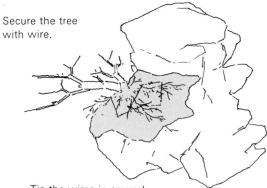

Tie the wires in several places as if making a net.

Thick roots should be fit into the hollow of the rock.

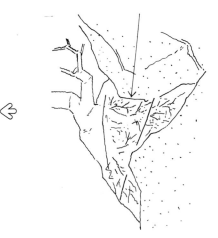

Sprinkle thoroughly with water.

When the tree is secure, press more peat muck around the base of the trunk and then cover the surface with moss. Anchor the moss with pins made of wire. The moss prevents the peat muck from flowing away and drying up, and also makes the bonsai look more mature.

If there appears to be a danger of dried soil pealing off, tie the tree and its root mass with polyethylene string until the roots grow and can hold the soil.

Place the tree and rock in a water tray. This looks attractive and has the advantage of helping to keep the tree moist.

Embracing Style

After the tree is attached to the rock, place it in a pot. Enclose the tree and rock with a piece of cardboard or a polyethylen sheet as shown, and fill with soil.

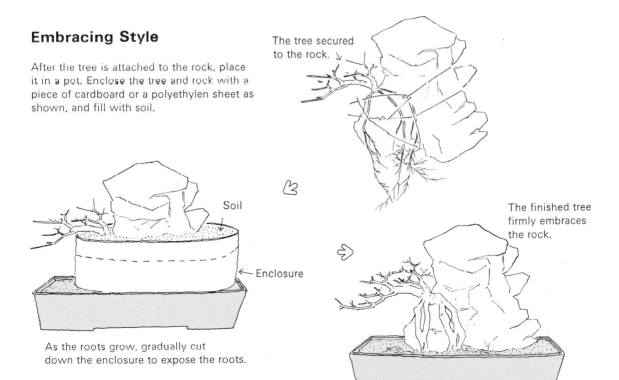

The tree secured to the rock.

Soil

Enclosure

As the roots grow, gradually cut down the enclosure to expose the roots.

The finished tree firmly embraces the rock.

Herbs and Grasses

In the wild, herbs and grasses grow without restriction, enjoying natural conditions. Once they are potted, however, they stop growing and the forms of the leaves become set. This contributes to the making of a good bonsai. Therefore, it is better to grow herbs and grasses in a small pot for one to two years after collecting them before planting them as bonsai.

Since they are grown in a small pot, it is not necessary to prune the roots and you can create the bonsai at any time regardless of the season. Herbs and grasses do not require any particular soil. In the example shown here, a mixture of sand and 20% red loam was used.

When you wish to repot, take the plants carefully out of the pot so as not to injure the roots. Remove the old soil with chopsticks, and then replant in the desired position in the pot. Repotting is necessary every two or three years.

A bonsai composed of herbs and grasses is quite different from that of trees, because the forms are completely natural and cannot be altered. The longer you grow them, however, the more interesting they become.

Herbs and grasses cultured in small pots for two to three years.

Pour soil in a flat container.

Remove old soil carefully with
a chopstick.

Planting.

The finished arrangement.

Index

Boldface numbers refer
to color photographs.

The back of the bonsai, 32
Bankan (coiled trunk), 27, **81**
Bankon (rock-like roots), 33
Broom style, 30
Buds, 66
Bunjingi (literati style), 27, **84**

Cascade style, 27, 93
Chokkan (formal upright style), 26, **73**
Clump, 29
Coiled style, 27
Crown, 95
Cuttings, 46

Dividing, 52

Eda-jin (weathered branch), 34
Equipment, 54
Exposed root, 29, 33
Extended branch, 30

Fertilizer, 64
Five-trunk, 28
Front of bonsai, 32
Formal upright style, 26
Fukinagashi (wind-swept style), 30
Futokoro-eda (bosomed branch), 35, 36

Gokan, (five-trunk), 28
Grafting, 50
Grasses, 104
Group planting, 31, 96

Han-kengai (semi-cascade style), **24**, 27
Hara-eda (belly branch), 36, 37
Herbs, 104
Hokidachi (broom style), **18**, 30

Ichi-no-eda (first branch), 35
Ikadabuki (raft style), 29
Imi-eda (undesirable branch), 35, 36
Informal upright style, 27
Ishitsuki (rock-grown), **15**, 31, **82**, 100

Jushin (apex), 35

Kabudachi (clump style), 29, **80**
Kannuki-eda (bar branches), 36, 37
Kasanari-eda (overlapping branches), 36, 37
Kata-nebari (one-sided root), 33
Kengai (cascade style), 27, **79**
Kuruma-eda (spoke-like branches), 36, 37

Layering, 48
Leaf cutting, 68
Literati style, 27

Mae-eda (front branch), 35, 36, 37
Moyogi (informal upright style), **13, 14, 17, 20, 21**, 27, **74, 75, 76, 78**

Neagari (exposed root style), 29
Nebari (root swelling), 33
Nejikan (twisted trunk style), 28
Netsuranari (sinuous root), **16**, 29
Ni-no-eda (second branch), 35

Ochi-eda (drooping branch), 35, 36

Pests, 65
Pinching buds, 66
Placement, 60
Pruning, 69

Raft style, 29
Repotting, 55
Rock-grown style, 31
Rock planting, 100

Sakasa-eda (opposing branch), 36, 37
Sankan (three-trunk), 28
San-no-eda (third branch), 35
Sashi-eda (extended, largest branch),
    30, 35, 36
Scion, 46
Seed, 44
Seedbed, 45
Seedlings, 39–43
Semi-cascade style, 27
Shakan, (slanting style), 27
Sharimiki (weathered trunk), 34
Single-trunk style, 28, 90
Slanting style, 27
Soils, 59
Sokan (twin-trunk style), 28, **83**
Shiho-happo nebari (roots growing in all
    directions), 33

Sinuous root, 29
Stock, 51

Tachiagari (lower part of the trunk), 34
Tankan (single-trunk style), 28
Ten-jin (weathered top), 34
Three-trunk style, 28
Tools, 54
Tsukidashi-eda (jutting branch), 36
Twin-trunk style, 28
Twisted trunk, 28

Uke-eda (counterbalance branch), 35, 36
Ura-eda (back branch), 35, 36

Watering, 62
Wind-swept style, 30
Wiring, 71

Yaku-eda (essential branch), 35
Yon-no-eda (fourth branch), 35
Yose-ue (group planting), **19**, 31, **77**, 96